JOB SEEKER'S WORKBOOK

Job Seeker's Workbook

For use with JIST's *Welfare-to-Work Video Series*

©2001 by JIST Publishing, Inc.

Published by JIST Works, an imprint of JIST Publishing, Inc.
8902 Otis Avenue
Indianapolis, IN 46216-1033
Phone: 1-800-648-JIST   Fax: 1-800-JIST-FAX
Web site: www.jist.com   E-mail: info@jist.com

IMPORTANT NOTE TO TRAINERS

The *Job Seeker's Workbook* was developed, written, and first published in 1998 by the International Training Academy (ITA) at the University of Colorado at Denver. The International Training Academy was established to meet the training needs of professional employment service providers, job developers, and career transition specialists. *Job Seeker's Workbook* was written to accompany the ITA's *World of Work Video Series*.

ITA thanks the following people and organizations for their assistance in the preparation of the *Job Seeker's Workbook:* Daniel Webster, Joe Lasky, Heather Bergman, Mercedes Bernal, Lance Noyes, Lisa Atencio, Ivy Carroll, Lisa Bobulinski, Jessica Spangler, Kristine Pedigo, and the staff of the National Veterans' Training Institute.

JIST Publishing edited the redesigned *Job Seeker's Workbook* into the present format and changed the name of the video series to the *Welfare-to-Work Video Series*. Each section of this workbook is named after and correlates to one video in the series. Therefore, the workbook must be used with the videos for maximum clarity and effectiveness. The workbook and the videos are available for purchase seperately from JIST. A seperate trainer's guide is included with the video.

Call 1-800-648-JIST or visit www.jist.com for a free catalog and for information on these and JIST's many other career-related products. Quantity discounts available.

Editor: Veda Dickerson
Cover and Interior Designer: Trudy Coler

Printed in the United States of America
07 06 05   9 8 7 6

ISBN 1-56370-833-7

About This Workbook

Job Seeker's Workbook is designed for use with JIST's *Welfare-to-Work Video Series*. It is organized into four easy-to-use sections, each matching one video in the series. Watch the four videos and complete the workbook exercises, and you will be on your way to finding and keeping a good job.

Your goal is to become independent and build your own success. With the help of the videos and this workbook, you will learn to

- Understand your financial needs and goals
- Recognize your job skills
- Identify your job interests and preferences
- Set goals
- Organize your job search
- Use various job-search tools
- Make contacts to discover available jobs
- Prepare for an interview
- Follow up after an interview
- Get ready for your first day on the job
- Be successful on the job

Table of Contents

SECTION
1

Getting Started

This section of your workbook can be used when you are ready to start looking for a job. It covers several topics.

- **Financial Needs:** You will determine how much money you need to earn right now and how much money you want to earn in the future.

- **Skills Identification:** You will learn what skills you have. These are skills you can offer to employers. You will think about what skills you want to use in your job.

- **Job Preferences and Interests:** You will identify where and how you prefer to work.

- **Goal Setting and Organization:** You will learn how to set short-term, intermediate, and long-term goals. You will learn to get organized by starting a Job-Search Portfolio. You will think about how to schedule your time and deal with the stresses that come with looking for a job.

FINANCIAL NEEDS

Your financial situation affects your career decisions. Early in your job search you must figure out how much money you need to survive. This will help you prevent financial disasters. You should look at both short- and long-term financial needs. You should look at your skills and how they relate to job requirements and pay scales. You should also think about how you will survive while attending school or getting training.

As you look at careers and jobs, compare your financial needs to the salaries of the jobs that interest you. You can find this information in the want ads of newspapers. You can also get this information by calling companies that have similar positions.

SAMPLE BUDGET

On page 4 is a *Sample Budget*. This page shows what your budget might be if you earn $5.15 per hour. It assumes that some expenses are paid, either completely or in part, by public assistance. The *Sample Budget* page also shows that when your hourly wage increases, you can increase your costs of living. The "Dream" column shows what your budget might be if your wages go up to $8.50 per hour.

BUDGET WORKSHEET

To identify your financial needs and set goals, complete the *Budget Worksheet* on page 5. Use your monthly expenses. Do not include income such as public assistance, disability, spouse's income, alimony, or student loans.

INSTRUCTIONS FOR COMPLETING THE BUDGET WORKSHEET

Step 1: Make sure every expense is listed. Add any missing items. You might consider including expenses such as eyeglasses, contact lenses, books, magazines, newspapers, public parking, vacations, cable TV, and spending money.

Step 2: Fill in the column that says "Needed to Get By," and total it. This is the amount of money you need to survive.

Step 3: Fill in the "Dream" column. Total it. This amount represents your goals.

Step 4: Calculate expenses such as payroll deductions, approximate federal and state tax, and retirement deductions. List the amounts in both columns.

HOURLY RATE: To find out what hourly rate you need, divide the amount of money you need each month by the number of working hours in the month (173). In the example, at the right, divide $891 (amount of money needed each month) by 173 (number of working hours in the month). This shows that you would need to make $5.15 per hour. Divide $1,472 by 173 to determine your dream needs. You would need to make $8.50 to reach your dream budget.

WEEKLY RATE: To find out what your weekly rate needs to be, multiply your hourly rate by the number of working hours in a week (40). In our example, the hourly rate you need to get by is $5.15. When you multiply that amount by 40, you see that you need to make $206 per week. When you multiply the dream rate of $8.50 by 40, you see that you need to make $340 per week to meet your dream budget.

MONTHLY RATE: To find what your monthly rate needs to be, multiply your hourly rate by the number of working hours in a month (173). In our example, the hourly rate needed to get by is $5.15. When you multiply that amount by 173, you see that you need to make $891 per month. When you multiply the dream rate of $8.50 by 173, you see that you need to make $1,470.50 per month to meet your dream budget.

YEARLY RATE: To find what your yearly rate needs to be, multiply your hourly rate by the number of working hours in a year (2,080). In the example, the hourly rate needed to get by is $5.15. When you multiply that amount by 2,080, you see that you need to make $10,712 per year. When you multiply the dream amount of $8.50 by 2,080, you see that you need to make $17,680 per year to meet your dream budget.

Sample Budget

Expense Area	Bills	Expenses	
		Needed to Get By	Dream
Residence	Rent	100.00	415.00
Electricity	Electricity		50.00
Telephone	Telephone		20.00
Meals	Groceries	200.00	200.00
	Eating Out		30.00
Transportation	Public Transportation	35.00	35.00
Insurance	Health	40.00	40.00
	Household	20.00	20.00
Personal	Barber and Beauty Shop		30.00
	Toiletries	30.00	30.00
	Day Care	250.00	250.00
Medical	Doctor	20.00	20.00
	Dentist	12.00	12.00
	Pharmacy	20.00	20.00
Clothing	Cleaning and Laundry	20.00	20.00
Recreation	Outings, Movies, etc.		20.00
Savings		+ 10.00	+ 40.00
Total	**Total Before Taxes & Deductions**	= $757.00	= $1,252.00
Payroll Deductions	Federal & State Taxes, Retirement, Social Security, etc.	+ 134.00	+ 220.00
Total Needed	**Total Necessary Monthly Income**	= $891.00	= $1,472.00

Budget Worksheet

Expense Area	Bills	Needed to Get By	Dream
		Expenses	
Residence	Rent		
Electricity	Electricity		
Telephone	Telephone		
Meals	Groceries		
	Eating Out		
Transportation	Public Transportation		
Insurance	Health		
	Household		
Personal	Barber and Beauty Shop		
	Toiletries		
	Day Care		
Medical	Doctor		
	Dentist		
	Pharmacy		
Clothing	Cleaning and Laundry		
Recreation	Outings, Movies, etc.		
Savings		+	+
Total	**Total Before Taxes & Deductions**	=	=
Payroll Deductions	*Federal & State Taxes, Retirement, Social Security, etc.	+	+
Total Needed	**Total Necessary Monthly Income**	=	=

HOURLY RATE: Amount you need, divided by 173 hours = _____ ÷ 173 = $_____/hour

WEEKLY RATE: Hourly Rate x 40 hours = $_____/week

MONTHLY RATE: Hourly Rate x 173 hours = $_____/month

YEARLY RATE: Hourly Rate x 2,080 hours = $_____/year

*Tax amounts change with income level. In the sample budget, taxes were figured at 17.7%. To determine the tax amount, multiply the Total amount by 17.7%. Add this amount to the Total to get the Total Needed:

$757 x .177 = $134 $757 + $134 = $891

As your income goes up, so will the amount deducted from your check for taxes, retirement, Social Security, and Medicare. To find out exactly what percentage of your check will be deducted for taxes and other programs, ask your employer.

SKILLS IDENTIFICATION

All skills have value in different jobs. Look at the list of skills below. Think about the specific tasks you did in your previous jobs. Think about the things you do at home. Think about what you did during the time you did not have a job. Think about what skills you have and what skills you want to improve.

INSTRUCTIONS FOR COMPLETING THE SKILLS INVENTORY

Step 1: Read the "Skill Area" column. Circle all your skills.

Step 2: Look at the "Rating Scale" and decide how you would rate your ability in each of the circled skills. Put the correct number under "Rating."

Step 3: Make a check mark under "Interest" to show what skills you want to use or develop in the future.

Step 4: If you have skills that are not listed, add them to the list.

Step 5: As you start thinking about jobs that interest you, use this list to see if you have the skills you would need in those jobs.

EXAMPLE		
Skill Area	**Rating**	**Interest**
Advised		
(Cataloged)	3	
Supervised		
(Wrote)	1	x

Skills Inventory

RATING SCALE

1 = Great   2 = Very good   3 = Good

Skill Area (example)	Rating	Interest
Adapted teaching style/special tools	_____	_____
Administered programs	_____	_____
Advised people/peers/job seekers	_____	_____
Analyzed data/blueprints/schematics/policies	_____	_____
Appraised services/value	_____	_____
Arranged meetings/events/training programs	_____	_____
Assembled automobiles/computers/apparatus	_____	_____
Audited financial records/accounts payable	_____	_____
Budgeted expenses	_____	_____
Calculated numerical data/annual costs/mileage	_____	_____

Skill Area (example)	*Rating*	*Interest*
Cataloged art collection/technical publications	_____	_____
Checked accuracy/other's work	_____	_____
Classified documents/plants/animals	_____	_____
Cleaned houses/auto parts	_____	_____
Coached teams/students/athletes	_____	_____
Collected money/information/data/samples	_____	_____
Compiled statistics/survey data	_____	_____
Confronted people/difficult issues	_____	_____
Constructed buildings	_____	_____
Consulted on a design configuration	_____	_____
Coordinated events/work schedules	_____	_____
Corresponded with other departments/colleagues	_____	_____
Counseled students/peers/job seekers	_____	_____
Created new programs/artwork/internet sites	_____	_____
Cut concrete/fabric/glass/lumber	_____	_____
Decided which equipment to buy/priorities	_____	_____
Delegated authority	_____	_____
Designed data systems/greeting cards	_____	_____
Directed administrative staff/theatre productions	_____	_____
Dispensed medication/information	_____	_____
Displayed results/products/artifacts	_____	_____
Distributed products/mail	_____	_____
Dramatized ideas/problems/plays	_____	_____
Edited publications/video tape/film	_____	_____
Entertained people/clients	_____	_____
Established objectives/guidelines/policies	_____	_____
Estimated physical space/costs/staffing needs	_____	_____
Evaluated programs/instructors/peers/students	_____	_____
Exhibited plans/public displays/evidence	_____	_____
Expressed interest in development projects	_____	_____
Facilitated multimedia exhibit/conflict resolution	_____	_____
Found missing persons/appropriate housing	_____	_____
Framed houses/pictures	_____	_____
Generated interest/support	_____	_____
Grew plants/vegetables/flowers	_____	_____
Handled detailed work/data/complaints/toxins	_____	_____
Hosted panel discussions/foreign students	_____	_____
Implemented registration system/new programs	_____	_____
Improved maintenance schedule/systems	_____	_____
Initiated production/changes/improvements	_____	_____
Inspected physical objects/repairs/electrical work	_____	_____
Installed software/bathrooms/electrical systems/parts	_____	_____
Interpreted languages/new laws/schematics/codes	_____	_____
Interviewed people/new employees	_____	_____

Skill Area (example)	Rating	Interest
Invented new ideas/machine parts	_____	_____
Investigated problems/violations/fraud	_____	_____
Landscaped gardens/public parks/indoor gardens	_____	_____
Led foreign tours/campus tours	_____	_____
Listened to others/to conference calls	_____	_____
Located missing information/facilities	_____	_____
Maintained transportation fleet/aircraft/diesel engines	_____	_____
Managed an organization/a mail room/a retail store	_____	_____
Measured boundaries/property lines/bridge clearance	_____	_____
Mediated between people/civil settlement	_____	_____
Met with dignitaries/public/community groups	_____	_____
Monitored progress of others/water flow/electric usage	_____	_____
Motivated workers/trainees	_____	_____
Negotiated contracts/sales/labor disputes	_____	_____
Operated equipment/hydraulic test stand/ robotics equipment	_____	_____
Organized tasks/library books/data bases	_____	_____
Painted houses/cars/aircraft/interiors	_____	_____
Patrolled runways/public places/property/buildings	_____	_____
Persuaded others/customers	_____	_____
Planned agendas/international conferences	_____	_____
Predicted future needs/stock market trends	_____	_____
Presented major selling points/new products	_____	_____
Prepared reports/meals/presentations	_____	_____
Printed books/reports/posters	_____	_____
Processed human interactions	_____	_____
Programmed computers	_____	_____
Promoted events/new products/new technology	_____	_____
Proofread news/reports/training materials	_____	_____
Protected property/people	_____	_____
Published reports/books/software	_____	_____
Purchased equipment/supplies/services	_____	_____
Questioned people/survey participants/suspects/ witnesses	_____	_____
Raised performance standards/capital investments	_____	_____
Read volumes of material/news releases	_____	_____
Recorded data/sales totals/music/video	_____	_____
Recruited people for hire/executives/Marines	_____	_____
Rehabilitated people/old buildings	_____	_____
Repaired mechanical devices/exhaust systems	_____	_____
Reported findings/monthly activity	_____	_____
Researched library documents/cancer/diseases	_____	_____
Renewed programs/contracts/insurance policies	_____	_____
Reviewed program objectives/books and movies	_____	_____

Skill Area (example)	*Rating*	*Interest*
Revised instructional materials	_____	_____
Scheduled social events/doctor's appointments	_____	_____
Sold advertising space/real estate/cars	_____	_____
Served individuals	_____	_____
Sewed parachutes/clothing/upholstery	_____	_____
Signed for the hearing impaired	_____	_____
Sketched charts and diagrams	_____	_____
Spoke in public	_____	_____
Supervised others	_____	_____
Taught classes/math/science	_____	_____
Tailored clothing/services	_____	_____
Televised conferences/training/events/shows	_____	_____
Tested new designs/students/employees	_____	_____
Updated files	_____	_____
Verified reports/identity	_____	_____
Volunteered services/time	_____	_____
Wrote reports/training manuals	_____	_____
Weighed trucks/patients/precious metals	_____	_____
Welded bike frames/airframes/alloys	_____	_____
X-rayed limbs/stressed equipment	_____	_____

Analyzing Your Skills

In the blanks below, list the skills you circled and checked in the *Skills Inventory*. Write an example of how you used that skill in your previous job.

EXAMPLE

Skill: Supervised
Example: Hired, trained, and evaluated a team of 10 retail sales people for 5 years

Skill:_____

Example:_____

Skill:_____

Example:_____

Skill:_____

Example:_____

Skill:_____

Example:_____

Skill:_____

Example:_____

Skill:_____

Example:_____

Skill:_____

Example:_____

Skill:_____

Example:_____

JOB PREFERENCES AND INTERESTS

The following survey will help you identify your job preferences and your interests. Keep this information in mind when you explore careers and companies. Your interests, your personal attitude, and your values should be suited to the jobs you decide to pursue.

Job Preferences and Interests Survey

Look at the 19 items on this page and the following page. For the 9 items on this page, circle the responses that best describe you. For the 10 items on the following page, write a short answer to each question.

1. I enjoy working with
   a. information, ideas, words, numbers
   b. people
   c. machines and equipment

2. I prefer working
   a. indoors
   b. outdoors
   c. some inside and some outside

3. I want to work for a company
   a. with less than 100 employees
   b. with 100 to 500 employees
   c. with 500 or more employees
   d. that I own

4. I would like to work in a
   a. large city
   b. medium-size city
   c. town or suburban area
   d. small town or rural area

5. I prefer a job that involves
   a. a lot of travel
   b. some travel
   c. no travel

6. I want a job that requires
   a. talking to a lot of people
   b. talking to people some of the time
   c. very little contact with other people
   d. no contact with other people

7. I would like work duties that
   a. change a lot
   b. change some from day to day
   c. change very little
   d. never change

8. I am willing to work overtime
   a. as much as possible
   b. often
   c. sometimes
   d. never

9. For the right job I am
   a. happy to move to another location
   b. willing to move to another location
   c. not able to move to another location
   d. not willing to move to another location

10. What are some things you like to do in your spare time?

11. What are your hobbies?

12. Are you more comfortable as a team member or as a team leader?

13. Where do you want to be doing 5 years from now?

14. Which of your past jobs did you like least? Why?

15. Which jobs did you like best? Why?

16. What kind of job would you do if you could choose any job you wanted?

17. Would you like to have more training? If so, what kind?

18. Why did you choose your previous field of work?

19. Using your responses to the items on this survey, how would you describe your most important work preferences?

> **EXAMPLE:** I prefer a job where I work with people. I want to be inside sometimes and outside sometimes. I want to work in a small city and do some traveling. I am willing to relocate, but not out of state.

I prefer a job where I:_____

Career Exploration

So far, you have looked at your financial needs, job skills, and work preferences. The closer these things match your job, the more likely you are to be successful and happy in that job.

Keep looking for your perfect job, but remember that you may not find an exact match between what you want and need and what is available.

Here is a list of ways you can explore careers:

- Do library research
- Receive employment counseling
- Contact the Small Business Administration
- Read business magazines
- Read the business section of newspapers
- Attend training or apprenticeship programs
- Talk to friends and relatives about work and careers
- Try a job-sharing arrangement
- Do informational interviews
- Get internships
- Make arrangements to shadow another person while he or she is at work (job shadow)
- Do volunteer work

INSTRUCTIONS FOR COMPLETING THE CAREER EXPLORATION FORM

On the next page, you will see a *Career Exploration Form*. List specific jobs you want to research and pursue. Refer to the worksheets you have already completed. You can also ask your friends, your family, or your case manager for ideas and suggestions.

Step 1: Identify jobs that interest you and write the titles on the following page.

Step 2: Research the salary range, necessary skills, and training/experience needed. Compare these to your own needs and skills.

Step 3: Look at each job you listed on the form. Ask yourself these questions: Am I over qualified, just right, or under qualified for this job? Does this job pay too little, just enough, or more than I need to survive?

Step 4: You may be ready to approach employers or you may want to explore new careers and jobs. You may want to get more training or education.

CAREER EXPLORATION FORM

JOB TITLE	SALARY RANGE	NECESSARY SKILLS	YOUR SKILLS	TRAINING/EXPERIENCE NEEDED
1. _____	$ _____			
2. _____	$ _____			
3. _____	$ _____			
4. _____	$ _____			
5. _____	$ _____			

GOAL SETTING AND ORGANIZATION

Deciding what you want to do and how to do it is an important part of setting goals. Your goals will vary depending on where you are in the job-search process.

When you set goals, think about what you want. Then think about what you need to do today, next week, next month, next year, and five years from now to get what you want. The job-search goals you set today will help you decide what actions you need to take.

You have already identified your financial needs and your job skills and preferences. You have thought about which jobs you will pursue. Now it's time to put it all together and set goals.

Keep in mind that a short-term goal for one person may be a long-term goal for someone else. For you, getting hired may be a short-term goal. For someone else who wants to go to school, getting hired may be a long-term goal.

EXAMPLES OF JOB-SEARCH GOALS

SHORT-TERM GOALS

- Identify my work preferences and financial needs
- Identify my job skills
- Identify careers and jobs that interest me; research the qualifications
- Compare my skills with the skills required for the job
- Decide which jobs I want to know more about
- Decide if I will get more education or training
- Begin my job search

INTERMEDIATE GOALS

- Continue exploring careers
- Schedule and structure my job search
- Develop resumes and cover letters; find job leads; get interviews
- Begin my education or training
- Get hired

LONG-TERM GOALS

- Complete my education or training
- Keep my job; improve my skills; move up

Setting Goals Worksheet

Look at the information you filled in on the other pages in this workbook. Think about your own personal and professional goals. Use the spaces below to record your goals. Think about ways to reach your goals. Add another sheet of paper if you need to.

SHORT-TERM GOALS

1._____

To fulfill this goal, I need to: _____

2._____

To fulfill this goal, I need to: _____

3._____

To fulfill this goal, I need to: _____

INTERMEDIATE GOALS

1._____

To fulfill this goal, I need to: _____

2._____

To fulfill this goal, I need to: _____

3._____

To fulfill this goal, I need to: _____

LONG-TERM GOALS

1._____

To fulfill this goal, I need to: _____

2._____

To fulfill this goal, I need to: _____

3._____

To fulfill this goal, I need to: _____

Job-Search Portfolio

A Job-Search Portfolio is a binder or other folder that holds all the information and documents you may need when applying for a job. It is also a great place to keep track of any calls or connections you make. Keeping an accurate, up-to-date, tidy Job-Search Portfolio will help you stay organized and on track as you send off resumes and complete applications.

To prepare your Job-Search Portfolio, collect the following information and documents and place them in a folder or binder:

Personal Records

You should include your driver's license, motor vehicle records, appropriate state or union licenses or certifications, social security card (the number is not enough, you need the card itself), birth certificate, and necessary work permits.

Master Application

You will find a sample master application on the following pages. Fill out the application completely. Refer to it when you fill out applications for jobs you are interested in.

Samples and Examples

You should include samples of your previous work; letters of recognition; personal and professional references; transcripts from schools or training programs you attended; and copies of honors, certificates, and diplomas you have received.

MASTER APPLICATION FOR EMPLOYMENT

_____ / _____ / _____
Date of Application

As an equal opportunity employer, this company does not discriminate in hiring or terms and conditions of employment because of an individual's race, creed, color, sex, age, disability, religion, or national origin.

AVAILABILITY

Position Applying for:_____   Date Available to Start:_____

Salary Desired:_____

Desired Schedule: Check Days Available: ☐ Sun   ☐ Mon   ☐ Tue   ☐ Wed   ☐ Thur   ☐ Fri   ☐ Sat

☐ Full-Time   ☐ Part-Time   ☐ Temporary   Hours Available Each Day: _____ _____ _____ _____ _____ _____ _____

PERSONAL INFORMATION

Last Name	First Name	Middle Name	
Present Street Address	City	State	Zip
Previous Street Address	City	State	Zip
Daytime Telephone No. ( )	Evening Telephone No. ( )	Social Security Number	Are you over 18?

EMPLOYMENT HISTORY

List employment starting with your *most recent* position. Account for any time during this period in which you were unemployed by stating the nature of your activities. If you have no prior employment history, include personal references to be contacted.

May we contact your present employer?   ☐ YES   ☐ NO

Employer	Dates		Position/Title
	From	To	
Address			Duties Performed
City State Telephone ( )			
Supervisor	Hourly Rate/Salary		
	Starting	Final	
Reason for Leaving			

Employer	Dates		Position/Title
	From	To	
Address			Duties Performed
City State Telephone ( )			
Supervisor	Hourly Rate/Salary		
	Starting	Final	
Reason for Leaving			

Employer	Dates		Position/Title
	From	To	
Address			Duties Performed
City State Telephone ( )			
Supervisor	Hourly Rate/Salary		
	Starting	Final	
Reason for Leaving			

Employer	Dates		Position/Title
	From	To	
Address			Duties Performed
City State Telephone ( )			
Supervisor	Hourly Rate/Salary		
	Starting	Final	
Reason for Leaving			

EDUCATION

Type of School	Name and Location of School		Degree / Area of Study	Number of Years Completed	Graduated? (check one)
High School	Name				☐ Yes ☐ No
	City	State			GPA_____
College	Name				☐ Yes ☐ No
	City	State			GPA_____
Other	Name				☐ Yes ☐ No
	City	State			GPA_____

SPECIAL SKILLS

☐ Typing   ☐ Lotus   ☐ Word Processing   ☐ 10 Key (by touch)   Applicable Skills or Equipment Operated:

_____wpm   _____keystrokes   _____

ACADEMIC AND PROFESSIONAL ACTIVITIES AND ACHIEVEMENTS

Academic and Professional Activities and Achievements, Awards, Publications, or Technical-Professional Societies. Indicate type or name. Exclude organizations which indicate race, creed, color, sex, age, religion, disability, or national origin of its members.	Date Awarded

MISCELLANEOUS

Is there any additional information involving a change of your name or assumed name that will permit us to check your record? If yes, please explain.

Have you ever been employed by this company or any of its divisions? ☐ Yes ☐ No	Dates Employed	Which Division?	Supervisor	Position

List names of friends or relatives now employed by this company.

Have you ever been convicted of a crime?   ☐ Yes ☐ No   (conviction of a crime does not automatically disqualify an applicant from consideration)
If yes, please explain:

Are there any jobs for which you do not wish to be considered? Please explain.

PERSON TO CONTACT IN CASE OF EMERGENCY

This information is to facilitate contact in the event of an emergency and is not used in the selection process.

Full Name	Address	Phone	Relationship to you?
Place of Employment	Address	Phone	

Scheduling Your Time

While you are looking for a job, you are your own boss. That means you have to manage your own time. Many successful job hunters schedule job-search activities eight hours a day, four days a week. Then, they take a day off to relax and reduce stress.

The first week of your job search should involve self-assessment and career exploration. Remember that your schedule will change week to week, and sometimes even day to day, as your job search progresses. Also, remember that you must be flexible in your scheduling and allow for interviews with prospective employers at any time.

One more thing to keep in mind is that you still need to stay on top of your household tasks (chores and bills). And don't forget to make time for relaxation and a little bit of fun!

On the next page, you will see a *Daily Schedule*. You may want to follow this example or use it as a guide for setting your own schedule.

DAILY SCHEDULE
WEEK ONE

MONDAY	TUESDAY	WEDNESDAY	THURSDAY	FRIDAY
Cold call 10 companies and record contacts	Cold call 10 companies and record contacts	Cold call 10 companies and record contacts	Set up informational interviews for next week	Day off, no job search activity
Read the business section of the newspaper	Research 10 companies at library	Read classified ads and business section of paper	Research 10 companies at library	Catch up on household chores
Contact 10 family members and friends	Work on resumes and cover letters	Respond to want ads	Go to human resources at A.B.C., Inc. and Acme, Corp.	Walk in park for one hour to relax
Register at local employment office	Go to chamber of commerce	Contact 10 previous coworkers	Play basketball to relax	
Follow up on want ads from Sunday's paper	Walk in park for one hour to relax			

Dealing With the Stresses of Looking for a Job

Being unemployed and looking for work can be extremely stressful. Some stress is normal, but there are things you can do to counteract negative stress.

Here are some suggestions for coping with job-search stress:

- **Get organized!** Use your Job-Search Portfolio, a date book, a personal phone book, your computer, and files.

- **Set a schedule.** Structure your time. Use a calendar to schedule your daily and weekly job-search activities.

- **Take time out for yourself.** Schedule time to do things you enjoy.

- **Join or develop a support group.** Groups are usually available through employment services, job clubs, churches, professional organizations, and community agencies. Get out and be with positive people. Help others, volunteer, network.

- **Schedule variety in your week.** Direct your job search in different areas and try new techniques.

- **Treat your job search like a real job.** Do not allow others to waste your time.

- **Exercise regularly and eat a balanced diet.**

- **Review your accomplishments each day.**

- **Expect rejection and do not take it personally.** Expect rejection from several employers before you get hired.

- **Prioritize your daily activities.** Make a list of important things to do.

- **Maintain important relationships.** Let family and friends know what you feel, but do not take your stress out on them.

SECTION

2

Your Job Is Out There

This section provides help with some very important job-search tasks. It covers these topics:

- **Job Search Tools:** You will learn to write a powerful resume and cover letter, and you will see examples of each. You will also receive valuable tips for filling out job applications.

- **Finding Work Opportunities:** You will discover techniques for finding an employer to whom you can submit your resume. You will learn to network, develop your telephone skills, respond to want ads, and research companies for which you might want to work.

JOB-SEARCH TOOLS

As you look for a job, you will need a well-written resume and cover letter, and you will need to know how to fill out an employment application. The first job-search tool we will look at is the resume.

Resume Guidelines

Following are some guidelines for writing a resume.

RESUME APPEARANCE

- Length usually should be one page but should never exceed two pages.

- Margins at top, bottom, left, and right should be 1 inch.

- Page should be easy to read and should include plenty of white space.

- Font size should be 10 or 12 and should be a conservative, easy-to-read style.

- Layout should be easy to follow, and information should be easy to locate.

- Appearance should be neat and clean, with no errors or corrections.

- Envelope and cover letter paper should match resume paper.

- Text should be left-justified with dates on the left.

- Print should be black.

RESUME CONTENT

- Show your previous responsibilities and results that relate to the needs of the company.

- Give examples of your accomplishments and your ability to solve problems.

- Show statistics and numbers.

- Be honest, positive, and specific.

- Use category headings such as Objective, Professional Highlights, Education, Training, Skills, Professional Associations and Organizations, Honors and Awards, and References.

- Avoid complete sentences; instead, use action verbs and other words with lots of impact.

- Include volunteer experiences, languages, internships, and certificates that relate to the position.

- Research the company and know what information would impress them.

- Use industry terminology when applicable.

GENERAL TIPS

- Write your own resume. Start by making a list of everything you've done—your work record, your education, and all your accomplishments.

- Leave off salary information. Provide it only when requested.

- Do not expect many results if you mass-mail your resume.

- Do not include postcards for employers to return.

- Use a computer or type your resume. Copy centers, libraries, schools, or local job-service centers may have the equipment you need.

- Do not provide names of references on the resume. Attach a reference sheet or provide references when requested.

- Mail your resume on a Tuesday or Thursday. Most people mail their resumes on Monday after they read the Sunday want ads or on Wednesday after they read the Wednesday want ads. Most of these resumes arrive on the same day—in a big pile! Mail your resume on a different day to help separate it—and you—from the rest of the pack.

RESUME FORMATS
WHICH ONE IS BEST FOR YOU?

RESUME FORMAT	WHAT'S GOOD ABOUT IT	WHAT'S BAD ABOUT IT	BEST USED BY
Functional - Shows what skills you have and what you can offer a company - Is organized by *skill*	- Looks at skills rather than employment history - Shows activities beyond employment, such as volunteer work and internships - Hides gaps in work record and frequent changes in jobs	- Makes employers suspicious because it does not offer a lot of information about specific employers - Hides skill development and job titles	- People with no previous employment - People with gaps in their employment record - Frequent job changers - People who have skills from activities other than employment
Chronological - Shows what jobs you have held and what tasks you performed at each - Is organized by *date*	- Is a widely used format - Is easy to read and very clear - Shows growth in skills and responsibility - Shows job growth and job titles - Shows company loyalty	- Shows gaps in employment - Highlights frequent job changes - Does not show skill development - Shows lack of related experience - Shows career changes - Points out career set-backs	- People with a steady work record - People with experience that relates directly to the position they are applying for
Combination - Explains where you have worked and what your skills are - First lists *skills* and then lists work history by *date*	- Shows most relevant skills - Combines skills developed in a variety of jobs or other activities - Takes focus away from drawbacks like gaps in employment and lack of experience	- Can be confusing if care is not taken to organize it well - Requires more effort and creativity to prepare	- People in transition or changing their careers - People re-entering the job market after being out for some time - People looking for work similar to what they've done in the past
Target - Is written with one company in mind - Can be based on any one of the other three formats	- Is specific to each company's needs - Shows that you have done research - Is more impressive to an employer	- Time-consuming to prepare - Can be confusing if care is not taken to organize it well - Must be revised for each employer	- Everyone, because any of the other resume formats can be made into a targeted resume

Mary Jenkins
301 Pearl Street, #15
Denver, Colorado 80204
Telephone: (303) 555-1111
mjenkins@resume.com

PROFESSIONAL OBJECTIVE

Administrative Assistant position where my coordinating, analyzing, planning, and budgeting skills would be utilized.

COORDINATING SKILLS

Coordinated fund-raising activities of 20 members of the local Parent Teacher Association (PTA), successfully raising $6,000 for playground facilities. As member of the Women's League of Rockville Methodist Church, initiated a relief center to meet clothing needs of the community. Also developed a schedule to meet demands of 5 busy household members, including arranging carpools, cleaning, cooking, and managing other general household duties.

BUDGETING SKILLS

As Treasurer of our local Civic Association, managed $10,000 budget for 2 years. Organized and managed family budget for 17 years. During this period, have accumulated savings necessary for 2 years of college for daughter. In addition to financial matters, have learned to budget time through efficient organization of community activities and family responsibilities.

COMMUNICATION SKILLS

Developed interpersonal skills during ten years' experience with PTA and church members. Learned the subtleties of persuading adults to contribute time and money to community projects. Invested considerable time and effort in developing open communication between family members. Mastered ability to retain sense of humor in tense situations.

MEMBERSHIPS

Elected treasurer of local Civic Association, 3-year term.
Voted to Board of Directors for Rockville Methodist Church, 1-year term.
President of PTA, 2 consecutive years.

REFERENCES

References furnished upon request.

Mark Peterson
5896 South Taylor Street
Lima, Massachusetts 60254

Home: (508) 333-6511 mpeterson@resume.com Office: (508) 555-4809

OBJECTIVE: Electrician with full range of responsibilities from maintenance to installation

SUMMARY: More than 12 years of experience in all phases of the electrical field. Expertise in troubleshooting electrical circuits and providing necessary maintenance. Effective supervisor of tradespeople.

EXPERIENCE

20XX—PRESENT **MASTER ELECTRICIAN**
XYZ Management Company, Lima, Massachusetts
- Total electrical renovation of apartments for new tenants: replaced fixtures, switches, receptacles, and wiring
- New wiring of single-family homes and town houses; commercial work on high-rise office buildings in the central Virginia area

20XX—20XX **ELECTRICIAN**
Walter Construction, Crinson, North Carolina
- Repaired, installed, adjusted, modified, and tested electrical systems and devices for 300,000 square feet of office and classroom space:
  - —Electrical Panels
  - —Fluorescent Lights
  - —Magnetic Starters
  - —Conduits
  - —Computers
  - —Switches and Receptacles
  - —Motors
  - —Breakers
  - —Incandescent Lights
  - —Ballasts
  - —Wire
  - —Telephone Lines
- Purchased material for over 1,000 electrical items
- Trained 2 apprentices on electrical maintenance procedures
- Supervised up to 4 tradespeople at varying times
- Read blueprints and schematics for wiring of new equipment, new additions, and new buildings
- Worked with voltages up to 480-volt, 3-phase systems

20XX—20XX **RETAIL CLERK**
Morgan's Pharmacy

EDUCATION

20XX—20XX Best Community College, Lima, Massachusetts
Courses focused on technical mathematics
Dean's List with 3.68 G.P.A.

20XX—20XX Training Community College, Old Harbor, Massachusetts
Electrical Construction—1,920 hours of study, certificate awarded 20XX

SPECIAL LICENSE

April 6, 20XX Massachusetts Journeyman's License #5678-JK

Judy Rogers
3678 St. George Ave. #31
Alameda, CA 90234
(141) 622-1111
jrogers@resume.com

Objective: Daycare Support Worker

Highlights of Qualifications
- Over 3 years of experience volunteering in a daycare setting
- Patient and caring when interacting with children of all ages and from all backgrounds
- Enthusiastic participant in children's games and educational activities
- Eager and effective member of working teams
- Well organized and able to handle multiple tasks simultaneously

Relevant Experience

Daycare/Working with Children
- Volunteered at my children's daycare 2 days each week for over 3 years
- Assisted in teaching Sunday School for toddlers at my family's church
- Room Mother for my son's first-grade class for 8 months
- Mother of three: two sons ages 3 and 6, one daughter age 4

Planning/Organization
- Created new enrollment record book for local daycare to make family contacts easier
- Participated in the development of Sunday School curriculum and activities for toddlers
- Coordinated children's contributions to class activities to ensure that all necessities are taken care of
- Managed a household of 5 people on a limited budget for more than 10 years

Volunteer and Work History

20XX—present	**Room Mother** Ms. Smith's First-Grade Class, Watkins Elementary School
20XX—present	**Volunteer** Tiny Tots Daycare Center
20XX—present	**Sunday School Volunteer** Sacred Heart Church
20XX—20XX	**Attendant** Clean as a Whistle Laundromat
20XX—20XX	**Babysitter** Jeffrey Dunn Family

References
- Available upon request

Jamie Donaldson
10 Emerson Drive
Lake Town, Virginia 33333
(101) 555-1234

Objective

Obtain a position as a Customer Service Representative for Swenson Software International

HIGHLIGHTS OF QUALIFICATIONS

- Two-years experience working in customer-service positions in computer industry
- Patient and effective when working with a wide range of personalities
- Successful in identifying and evaluating computer-related problems

RELEVANT EXPERIENCE

Customer Relations

- Processed 120 telephone orders for hardware and software every day
- Initiated new 6-step procedure for completing customer orders that decreased on-phone time by 50 percent
- Responded to customer comments; resolved or referred all customer complaints within 24 hours

Telecommunications

- Accepted or redirected 250 in-bound, customer telephone calls every day
- Managed telephone system with 35 lines and 12 extensions, without complication
- Recorded customer-contact and sales data in daily telephone log

Computer Usage

- Entered and updated customer orders in appropriate computer databases
- Researched hardware and software information in response to customer inquiries
- Compiled weekly sales reports for telesales division

Problem Solving

- Tracked down and corrected misdirected customer orders
- Reorganized telesales workspace to increase working efficiency and productivity
- Created new timesheets and employee rosters to clarify information related to hours worked and vacation taken

EMPLOYMENT HISTORY

20XX—20XX	**Customer Service Representative**	LAM Computers, Lake Town, VA
20XX—20XX	**Customer Service Assistant**	Executive Technologies, Pleasantown, VA
20XX—20XX	**Telemarketing Associate**	Donzall & Associates, Monton, VA
20XX—20XX	**Cashier**	Don Roberto's Cafe, Monton, VA
20XX—20XX	**Cashier**	McDonald's, Monton, VA

EDUCATION

Coursework in Business Marketing	Norwest College, Santa Rosa, VA

Action Words

Look at the words in the list below. Find the ones that best describe your knowledge and skills. Use them on your resume, job applications, and cover letters.

Be sure you know the definition of each word before you use it. If you are unsure of the meaning of a word, look it up in a dictionary. Choose your words carefully, and be sure you use them correctly.

Remember: Your application, cover letter, and resume are all reflections of you and your abilities. Make them look and sound as good as you can without being deceptive or misleading.

achieved	advocated	appraised	assigned
adapted	allocated	arbitrated	assisted
addressed	analyzed	arranged	attended
administered	applied	assembled	audited
advised	appointed	assessed	
balanced	budgeted	built	
calculated	collated	composed	contributed
changed	collected	computed	controlled
clarified	communicated	conceptualized	coordinated
classified	compared	conducted	corrected
coded	compiled	consolidated	counseled
collaborated	completed	consulted	created
debated	designated	developed	dispersed
decreased	designed	diagnosed	displayed
defined	detailed	directed	distributed
delegated	determined	discovered	drafted
demonstrated			
edited	engaged	examined	expanded
educated	ensured	exceeded	expedited
enabled	equipped	executed	experimented
encouraged	established	exercised	explained
enforced	estimated	exhibited	expressed
facilitated	fixed	formulated	funded
filed	focused	founded	
gathered	generated	guided	

Action Words (*continued*)

helped   hired

identified	increased	installed	interviewed
illustrated	influenced	instituted	introduced
implemented	informed	instructed	invented
improved	initiated	integrated	investigated
improvised	inspected	interpreted	involved
incorporated	inspired		

justified

learned	led	lobbied	located
lectured			

maintained	marketed	moderated	monitored
managed	mediated	modified	motivated
mapped	mobilized		

observed	operated	organized	originated
obtained	ordered		

packaged	planned	produced	proposed
participated	prepared	programmed	provided
perceived	presented	projected	publicized
performed	prioritized	promoted	published
persuaded	processed	proofread	purchased
photographed	procured		

qualified

raised	recruited	reorganized	researched
reasoned	redesigned	repaired	restored
received	reduced	replaced	restructured
recognized	reevaluated	reported	reviewed
recommended	referred	represented	revitalized
recorded	refined	reproduced	rewrote

scheduled	shaped	started	summarized
screened	simplified	stocked	supervised
selected	sold	structured	supported

Action Words (*continued*)

separated	solicited	studied	surpassed
served	solved	submitted	surveyed
serviced	staffed	succeeded	synthesized
set	staged	suggested	systematized
tabulated	terminated	trained	transported
tailored	testified	translated	traveled
taught			
updated	utilized		
validated	verified	visualized	
wrote			
x-rayed			

_____

_____

_____

_____

Jacob Roberts
123 Treefront Street
Des Moines, IA 12345
(123) 456-7899

REFERENCE SHEET

PROFESSIONAL REFERENCES

Julia Silvers, Administrative Manager
Kent Products, Inc.
123 West 32nd Street
Des Moines, IA 12345
(123) 111-2222

Robert Williams, Department Manager
Spruce Electronics
1234 Jefferson Avenue
Des Moines, IA 12345
(123) 998-7654

Joseph Mitchell, Director of Marketing
Jones Imports
12 Wheeling Circle
Des Moines, IA 12345
(123) 222-1111

PERSONAL REFERENCES

Joy Smith
2345 East Park
Hanover, IA 12345
(111) 131-3131

Jason McMurphey
11 Market Street
Des Moines, IA 12345
(123) 554-9901

NOTE: Always contact your references before including them on your Reference Sheet.

Writing a Cover Letter

Read and follow these guidelines when preparing a cover letter. Remember to keep a copy of every cover letter you send out.

Your cover letter:

- Is a sales pitch and an attention-getter

- Identifies the single most important reason why you should get further consideration for the job

- Should allow the reader to make a connection with your background

- Identifies mutual friends or company employees you know

- Expresses your knowledge of the company

- Is a personal communication between you and the employer

- Does not repeat, but can highlight, information in your resume

- Is short and to the point—no more than half a page

- Mentions why you would like to work for the company

- Uses perfect grammar and spelling

- Identifies relocation issues

- Is the first impression an employer has of you, so should be good

General Outline for a Cover Letter

[Your Name]
[Your Street Address]
[Your City, State, Zip Code]

[Date of Letter]

[Employer's Name]
[Employer's Title]
[Company Name]
[Company Street Address]
[Company City, State, Zip Code]

Dear [Employer's Name]:

[INTRODUCTION PARAGRAPH: You want to tell the reader why you are writing and which position you are applying for. You also want to get the reader's attention. Mention how you heard about the organization or the opening. Name someone you and the reader both know or someone in the company who knows you. Show you've done some research on the company. Talk about new projects the company has taken on or the company's management philosophy, or cite something you've read about the company.]

[BODY: In this section, you want to build a connection between your background and the company's needs. Sum up your related experience or education so the reader can look for it in your resume. If you have skills or accomplishments that relate to the job, mention them here. You are effectively summarizing your skills as they relate to the company. Do this with confidence.]

[CONCLUDING INFORMATION: State your interest in working for the company and hearing from the reader. Thank the reader for his/her time and consideration.]

Sincerely,

[Your Signature]

[Your Name Typed]

Enclosure

James Donaldson
10 Emerson Drive
Capetown, Florida 33333
(101) 555-1234

July 12, 20XX

Ms. Mary Smith
Personnel Director
Add It Up
5678 East Doral Street, Suite #1200
Lockridge, Tennessee 77777

Dear Ms. Smith:

In response to your ad in the *Lockridge Examiner* dated January 8, 20XX, I am enclosing my resume for consideration. I was particularly attracted to the clerical position you advertised, because I am interested in accounting and have strong secretarial skills. I am excited about the opportunity to use these skills to work for a firm like Add It Up, which has been a leader in accounting systems for many years and shows great promise for growth in the future.

I have extensive experience and skills that are relevant to the clerical position. I am skilled in budgeting, invoicing, and billing, and I am able to perform all major secretarial tasks. I am friendly and enthusiastic both on the phone and in person. This makes me a good person to work with and enables me to relate well to customers. I am certain my talents would be valuable to Add It Up, a company with a strong focus on customer service.

I believe I would be a good candidate for the clerical position you are seeking to fill, and I look forward to hearing from you soon.

Sincerely,

James Donaldson

James Donaldson

Enclosure

Maria L. Griego
765 Williams Lane
Chicago, IL 99999
(555) 111-1111

March 15, 20XX

Mr. R. L. Montrose
Department Manager
Manos/Hands
222 Drawbridge Road
New York, NY 24680

Dear Mr. Montrose:

In response to your ad for a Spanish Language Translator in the *Chicago Tribune* dated September 14, 20XX, I am enclosing my resume for your consideration.

I was particularly attracted to the translator position because of my interest in social issues and because of my own Spanish background. The position also appealed to me because it offers the opportunity for me to use my language skills and communications experience to help improve the lives of people in depressed urban areas.

I have an excellent command of both Spanish and English, as well as an understanding of poverty and Latino issues. Additionally, I have a big heart and am eager to put my skills to use.

I believe I would be a good candidate for your position as a Spanish Language Translator and look forward to hearing from you soon.

Sincerely,

Maria Griego

Maria L. Griego

Enclosure

Jane Doe
876 Foothills St.
Denver, CO 65656

February 15, 20XX

Mrs. Kathy Smith
Tiny Tots Daycare
4545 Main Street
Denver, CO 65656

Dear Mrs. Smith:

It was a pleasure to spend the day with you and the children at Tiny Tots Daycare last week.

It was very interesting to me to see the fun and educational games you were playing with the children. I was also very pleased to see that you set aside quiet time for the little ones, but did not insist that everyone sleep. I think teaching children to be quiet and respectful of others is important, and I was glad to see that this behavior is taught at Tiny Tots.

I also found our discussion during lunch very helpful. I appreciate all the information you gave me about both the good and the bad aspects of working in daycare. As I mentioned to you, I have volunteered at a daycare for a few years now, and I have found that there is much more good than bad in this profession!

I would be thrilled to work with you at Tiny Tots and to contribute to the education and care of those wonderful children. I have enclosed my resume for your review. I think you will find that creativity and enthusiasm are my strengths, and those traits come in handy when working with children. Thank you very much for your time and kindness. I look forward to hearing from you soon.

Sincerely,

Jane Doe

Jane Doe

Enclosure

Applications

Employers usually will ask you to complete an application form instead of, or in addition to, giving them your resume. Use your completed *Master Application for Employment* from Section 1 for help when you are filling out an application.

Be careful of the words you use to describe your situation. If the employer is interested in what you have been doing or why you left your last job, he or she can ask for more information during your interview. You can answer the employer's questions at that time.

NEVER WRITE:	INSTEAD WRITE:
Was fired	Will discuss during interview
Hated my boss	Had personality conflict
Got pregnant	Stayed home to raise family
Bummed out	Made career shift
Had a dead-end job	Left to seek employment with more career opportunities
Was on public assistance	Will discuss in interview
Never worked	(Describe any volunteer work you have done or other activities you have been involved in.)

Acceptable reasons for leaving a job:

- To further your education (use only once in your work history)
- To make a career change
- To raise a family (use only once in your work history)
- To relocate
- Because of work-force reduction (laid off)
- Because of seasonal work (laid off)
- For better growth opportunity
- Because job was temporary

Any of these statements are acceptable for reporting your work history. But remember that lying or misleading a potential employer is always a bad idea. Be honest. If these statements don't apply to your situation, don't use them.

PREPARING A GREAT-LOOKING APPLICATION

When you are given an application to fill out, ask if you can take it home and complete it there. If so, take the application to a grocery store or copy center and make a photocopy. Or, ask the employer for an extra copy of the application. Either way, if you make errors on the original application, you'll have an extra copy. When you return the application to the employer, it will be neat.

Bring white-out with you in case the employer prefers that you complete the application in the office. Applications must be filled out in pen. Using white-out is the best way to make sure your work is tidy and professional. Your application reflects your abilities, so make it look great!

Jacob Roberts
123 Treefront Street
Des Moines, IA 12345
(123) 456-7899

SALARY HISTORY

Grazier International
123 Alameda Avenue
Des Moines, Iowa 12345
20XX—20XX
Position Range: $21,500—$24,000/year, plus excellent benefits

Balvin Corporation
456 Westcliff Street
Council Bluffs, Iowa 12345
20XX—20XX
Position Range: $20,000—$21,000/year, plus health & vacation benefits

Computer Resources Inc.
135 Jenson Avenue
Council Bluffs, Iowa 12345
20XX—20XX
$20,000/year

**NOTE: Only provide a
salary history when it is
requested by an
employer.**

FINDING WORK OPPORTUNITIES

This section will help you learn to tap into the job market, including the hidden job market. To do this, think about the hiring process from the employer's point of view.

The hiring process often looks like this:

- A job opening exists.

- The people in a position to hire go to their *internal networks.* They may hire or promote someone who already works for the company. They may encourage people they know to apply. They may look at resumes or applications they've already received. In large companies, they may go to the Human Resources Department to look for qualified applicants. Jobs are often filled at this point.

- Large companies and government agencies usually post job openings and announce jobs through *external networks* such as professional groups, job hot lines, and job boards. Some companies use an outside *placement agency* if they do not have a Human Resources Department.

- Employers usually place *a want ad* if they can not fill a job using any other method.

Your job is to get yourself, your resume, and your job application into the employer's internal network. You should still contact friends, relatives, and previous coworkers; and you should still check with placement agencies and search the want ads. But an employer's internal network, also called the hidden job market, is where most hiring takes place.

NOTE: Even if a job opening appears in the want ads, someone in the employer's internal network often gets hired. These people have the inside track on job openings. Also, many employers place want ads to meet legal requirements or to build up a pool of qualified applicants, yet still hire people from their internal network. This may be frustrating for the job seeker, but it is often the way things are done.

JOB-SEARCH METHODS

People use a variety of methods to find information about job openings. Some read the want ads; others ask friends or relatives; and still others contact employers directly. Successful job seekers use a wide variety of methods but focus most of their time and energy on the more-effective methods.

Refer to the chart on the following page. Consider the advantages and disadvantages of some of the more-common methods used by job seekers.

Method	Advantages	Disadvantages
Want Ads	Easily accessed, delivered to home or newsstand	Contains only 15% of job openings Employers use as a last resort
Mass-Mailing Resumes	You may get lucky	5% or lower response rate to resumes sent blind to a company or personnel department
Targeted Resume	Sending a resume to a specific person will increase your chances of an interview Contacting an employer and then sending a resume is most effective	This is time consuming and takes a lot of research
Personal Contacts and Cold Calling	75% of all jobs are found through these two methods of networking	Requires excellent telephone and communication skills Is time consuming

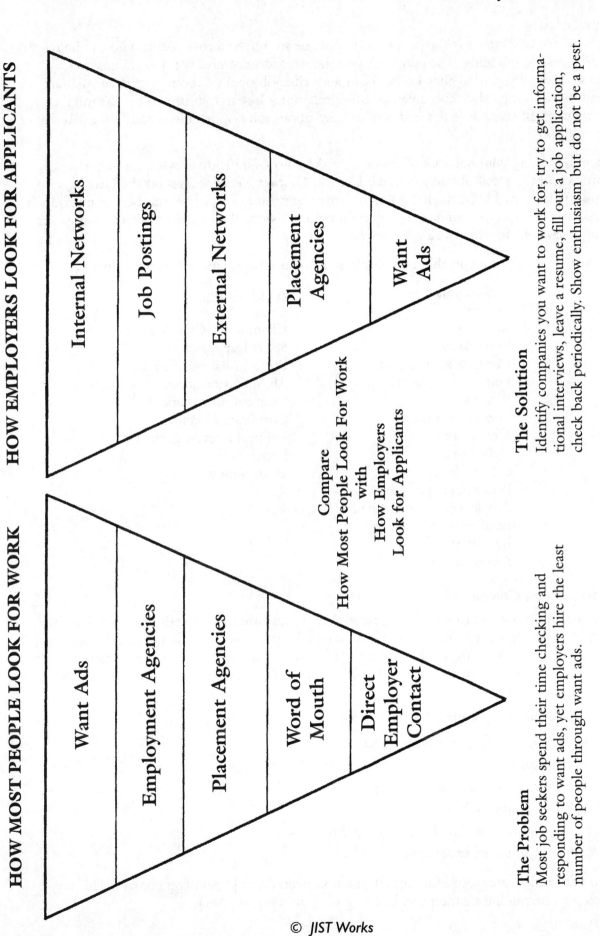

HOW MOST PEOPLE LOOK FOR WORK

- Want Ads
- Employment Agencies
- Placement Agencies
- Word of Mouth
- Direct Employer Contact

HOW EMPLOYERS LOOK FOR APPLICANTS

- Internal Networks
- Job Postings
- External Networks
- Placement Agencies
- Want Ads

Compare
How Most People Look For Work
with
How Employers
Look for Applicants

The Problem
Most job seekers spend their time checking and responding to want ads, yet employers hire the least number of people through want ads.

The Solution
Identify companies you want to work for, try to get informational interviews, leave a resume, fill out a job application, check back periodically. Show enthusiasm but do not be a pest.

Judith M. Hoppin at the Oakland University in Rochester, Michigan developed the information on this page.

Networking

Your network of contacts is the people you know or are referred to—people who can help you identify possible job leads. The people in your network do not give you jobs themselves. Instead, they tell you what they know about a specific job field or about companies that are expanding or hiring. They also give you other relevant job-search information. Creating a large network of contacts is the best way to learn about job opportunities and find a job that works for you.

To begin building your network of contacts, make a list of individuals who can help you research companies and obtain job leads. Use the *Contact Network Sheet* on the next page to organize your network. In the left column, write the names and phone numbers of individuals and associations you will contact. In the right column, write the names of people, companies, and organizations to which you are referred.

The list below will help you think of people and organizations you may want to include.

Individuals	**Associations**
Friends	Church
Relatives	Chamber of Commerce lists
Coworkers	Sport leagues
Clients and customers	Professional associations
Former employers	Alumni associations
Bankers	Convention rosters
Friends of friends	Corporate directories
Merchants	Political interest groups
Neighbors	Social clubs
Other job seekers	Trade shows
Personnel departments	
People already in the field	
Landlords and realtors	
Recruiters	
School contacts	

QUESTIONS FOR CONTACTS

Many people do not like to network because they do not want to advertise the fact that they are unemployed. If networking bothers you, remember that you are not asking the people in your network for a job. You are just letting them know that you are looking for work and that you need information. Most people will not have a job to offer, but they will have valuable information to share.

Ask your contacts some questions to find out

- What they know about a certain career
- Who they know
- Who they can introduce or refer you to
- Which companies are hiring
- What the future looks like for the occupation
- Which companies are expanding

Try to get at least one piece of useful information from every person you contact. This way you keep gathering information and building your network of contacts.

Contact Network Sheet

Personal contacts, such as friends, relatives, or associates	Companies and contact persons I have been referred to
Example:	
Jim Johnson at Elks Club referred me to	*Sue Peterson at Kacey Electrical Contractors (808) 123-4567*

Telephone Skills

The telephone is a great tool for obtaining job leads and information about jobs and companies. Many people feel uncomfortable calling strangers. They fear rejection and are afraid they will get tongue-tied when they have a potential employer on the line.

This section will help you become more effective in using the telephone to find a good job.

COLD CALLING FOR INFORMATION

Chances are that the people you call do not get a lot of calls from job seekers. Treat them as experts in their fields, and do so in a friendly manner. They will probably be pleasant, and they might even be flattered that you are seeking their advice. Be brief and specific about the purpose of your call. You can get information about a particular occupation or company, or details about what it takes to qualify for a certain job. Also, as you talk to more and more people, you will develop an overall understanding of the industry you are researching.

A cold call may lead to a visit to the company and an informational interview. These can be valuable experiences and in some instances may lead to a job.

MAKING PRACTICE CALLS

You may be worried about getting tongue-tied while you are on the phone with someone you really want to work for. If so, try calling people at companies you do not want to work for. Practice asking them about their industry, about the equipment and technology they use, and about the job qualifications, hiring practices, and trends in their industry. Write down information as you speak to them. This will help you get used to taking notes while on the phone. By making practice calls, you will become familiar with industry terminology. You might be surprised at how much people are willing to tell you about their work.

CONTACTS THAT COUNT

Getting through to the right person is sometimes difficult. So remember—

- Be courteous and businesslike with everyone
- Convey confidence that your call will reach its goal
- Expect the receptionist to ask who you are and who and what you want
- Ask for the appropriate manager and, if you don't already know the person's name, try to get it before you are transferred
- Ask when is a good time to call back, if your contact is not available
- Leave a message if you absolutely cannot get through
- Prepare an outline or script

Here is an example of what you might say.

"Good afternoon. My name is _____. May I speak with your
_____ [production, marketing, design, construction, etc.] manager?"

"What is the purpose of the call?"

"I'm looking for information about that department, and I was referred by
Mr./Ms. _____."

When your call gets through

- Use your outline or script

- Introduce yourself and mention who referred you

- Give a brief description of your interests and background

- Have a list of topics and questions you want to discuss

You might say, "I'm looking for work in the _____ field, and I'd like your advice. I know you're busy, but I'd appreciate it if you could spare just 10 minutes."

When the person is willing to talk

- Ask questions like these:

    What qualifications do people who work in this position have?

    What qualifications do entry level people have?

    I am planning to attend _____ school. Have you ever hired anyone who attended that school?

    How many _____ [job title] work in your department?

    When you have an opening for _____ [job title], how tough is the competition?

    How many people have you hired in the last six months?

    What type growth do you project for your industry?

- Ask for the name and number of someone else who works in the same field.

- Ask if you can stop by to ask a few more questions.

- Take notes during the call. Afterward, update your contact sheet.

Example Contact Sheet

On this page, you have an example of a completed *Contact Sheet*. You can use a *Contact Sheet* to write down company information, the date of your contact, key points about the contact, and follow-up information. Be specific.

You can copy the blank *Contact Sheet* on the next page and use it for your own company contacts.

COMPANY: Air Quality Inc.
ADDRESS: 1122 S. Broadway, Denver, Colorado
TELEPHONE: (303) 893-2126
CONTACT PERSON/TITLE: John Jamison, Air Quality Manager

DATE	ACTIVITY/RESULTS	FOLLOW-UP
04/01/20XX	Cold call at 10 a.m. Receptionist said company has 300 employees. Spoke with Human Resources. They told me to speak to Mr. Jamison, Design Department Supervisor.	Call back to Mr. Jamison on 04/03/20XX
04/03/20XX	Spoke with Mr. Jamison. Set up informational interview for 04/10/20XX. Personable, but very busy. Spoke for only 5 minutes.	04/10/20XX, 7:30 a.m.
04/10/20XX	Met with Mr. Jamison. He said that in the next 3 months the industry will need many smog-certified mechanics due to new laws. Must be certified! Recommended I call Carol Dey, Installation Supervisor at Air Quality, Inc.	Call Carol Dey
04/15/20XX	Spoke to Carol Dey. She said to send her a resume. Sent resume and cover letter today.	Check back with Carol Dey on 04/20/20XX

Contact Sheet

COMPANY:
ADDRESS:
TELEPHONE NUMBER:
CONTACT PERSON, TITLE:

DATE	ACTIVITY/RESULTS	FOLLOW-UP

Responding to Want Ads

Want ads announce job openings in the classified sections of newspapers and certain industry publications. Some job seekers do find employment by responding to want ads. Looking through want ads can give you a good idea of what jobs are available in various industries. You may be able to get information on what experience, qualifications, and skills you need and what salary you can expect. Job openings may exist in a certain field even though no specific positions are listed in the want ads.

Most ads first appear on Wednesday or Sunday, so pay attention on those days. Read all of the want ads, because jobs that interest you may be listed in unexpected places. For example, want ads for drywallers may be listed under construction, painters, laborers, home builders, carpenters, or other job categories.

When reading and responding to want ads be aware of the following:

- Some ads list a post office box instead of a company name. This prevents you from doing any research on the company.

- Ads that promise a big paycheck usually are for sales positions which involve working on commission.

- If the contact for the ad is an employment agency, find out if they will charge you a fee. Some agencies charge the employer a fee; some charge the job seeker a fee.

- Multiple-position ads usually indicate a new or expanding company. Many people will be competing for these positions.

- Some ads use the word "preferred," as in "degree preferred" or "two-years experience preferred." This usually means you can apply even if you do not have that particular skill or ability, if you do have the other qualifications.

- Be sure you meet the minimum requirements listed in the want ad. If it says that certification, license, degree, or experience are required, you will probably be wasting your time applying if you do not have those qualifications. If the ad says "no phone calls," do not call.

Abbreviations in the Want Ads

acctg...........accounting
accts...........accounts
a/p...........accounts payable
a/r...........accounts receivable
admin...........administrative
adv...........advertise/advertising
ad...........advertisement
AA...........Affirmative Action
agen...........agency
appl...........application
appt...........appointment
asst...........assistant
ASAP...........as soon as possible
avail...........available
ben...........benefits
bkpr...........bookkeeper
bkpg...........bookkeeping
cap (or cap inv)...........capital investment
cert...........certificate/certified
comm...........commission
co...........company
compat...........compatible
comp...........computer
conf...........conference
corp...........corporation
DP...........data processing
deg...........degree
del...........delivered
DOE...........depends on experience
dev...........develop/developed/developing
dir...........director
div...........division
educ...........education
empl...........employment
engr...........engineer
EOE...........Equal Opportunity Employer
exc...........excellent
exec...........executive
exp/exper...........experience
flex...........flexible
FT...........full-time
gen/genl ofc...........general office
grad...........graduate
HS...........high school
hosp...........hospital
hskpg...........housekeeping
immed...........immediate
incl...........includes/including
ind/indust...........industrial
info...........information
inq...........inquire
install...........installation
inst...........institute
ins...........insurance

lab...........laboratory
ldscpg...........landscaping
lndry...........laundry
lic...........licensed
mach...........machine
maint...........maintenance
mgmt...........management
mgr...........manager
mfgr...........manufacturer
mfg...........manufacturing
mkt...........market
mech...........mechanic/mechanical
med...........medical
mb...........megabits
mhz...........megahertz
mdse/merch...........merchandise
min...........minimum
mtg...........mortgage
nego...........negotiable
oper...........operate/operator
PT...........part-time
perm...........permanent
PC...........personal computer
persn'l...........personnel
phone/ph...........telephone/telephones
pos...........position
prefd...........prefer/preferred
pres...........president
proc...........process/processing/processor
prof...........professional
prog...........programmer
PR/pub rel...........public relations
purch...........purchasing
qual...........qualify
recept...........receptionist
refs...........references
reqd...........required
sal...........salary
secy...........secretary
SASE...........self-addressed stamped envelope
ship/rec...........shipping and receiving
shnd...........shorthand
std...........standard
steno...........stenographer
ste...........suite
supvr...........supervisor
tech...........technical/technician
temp...........temporary
transp...........transportation
univ...........university
voc...........vocational
whse...........warehouse
whsle...........wholesale

Researching the Company

Create a list of companies where you would like to work. Prioritize the list and spend your time researching these companies.

Look for information about the company in libraries, in book stores, at college career centers, or at your State Department of Labor.

Information to research before contacting a company:

- The number of employees

- What the company does—their services and/or products

- The company's competitors

- The company's history and future plans

- The company's locations—headquarters, branch offices, international offices, and retail outlets

- The salary range or hourly rates paid for various positions

- Contact names—department heads, the Human Resources Manager, people you know who work there, and former employees

- Employment activity—recent hirings, firings, or layoffs

- Titles of positions that interest you

As you research companies, keep a record of important information on the *Company Research Worksheet* on the following page. Keep this information organized and easily accessible. Fill out one worksheet for each company you research.

Company Research Worksheet

List everything you already know about the position or company, including duties, salary, location, and company size.

Make a list of questions you want answered before approaching the company, such as who has hiring authority and what the company's current projects are.

Company Information Record

Use this form to keep track of the companies you research. Ask your librarian how to get information on specific companies. The business section of newspapers, the Chamber of Commerce, trade journals, Job Service Centers, and professional associations are other great sources of information. Also, record any information you get from cold calls and informational interviews.

Organization name:_____

Address:_____

Phone:_____ Position of interest:_____

Required skills, certification, education, work experience:_____

_____

Types of services and/or products:_____

Names and phone numbers of possible contact people:_____

_____

Owners/President:_____ Phone:_____

Foreman/Supervisor:_____ Phone:_____

Manager:_____ Phone:_____

Personnel Officer:_____ Phone:_____

General reputation of industry:_____

Source and date of information:_____

Date, person phoned, results:_____

Pertinent information about the company, such as new contracts or products, expansions, hirings, layoffs, lawsuits, competitors, stock prices, plans for the future, and number of employees:_____

_____

_____

SECTION

3

Making a Good Impression

This section will help you handle job interviews. It covers these topics:

- **Preparing for an Interview:** You will think about what you should and should not do when interviewing for a new job. You will consider how your appearance—clothing and grooming—affects the success of your interview. You will learn the importance of preinterview preparations.

- **Following Up After an Interview:** You will learn to write an appropriate follow-up note to the person who interviewed you. You will look at a post-interview checklist and think about some ways you can learn from your interview experience.

PREPARING FOR AN INTERVIEW

The time you spend getting ready for a job interview can have a great impact on whether you get the job.

Hints for a Successful Interview

IT'S A GOOD IDEA TO...

- Bring only essential items to the interview; for example, resume, references, portfolio, licenses, and date book.

- Arrive 15 minutes early so you can relax and review what you want to say.

- Be pleasant and friendly but businesslike to everyone you meet.

- Shake hands firmly. Be yourself. Use natural gestures and movements.

- Stress your qualifications and emphasize experience and training related to the job opening.

- If you know about the company's products and services, refer to them as you answer questions. Your positive knowledge of the company will be impressive.

- After being asked a question, pause and think think about your answer. Answer questions with more than a yes or no. A successful interview occurs if the interviewer talks 50 percent of the time.

- Speak positively about past employers. Stress what was good about previous work experiences, even if you were unhappy with the way things turned out.

- Talk positively about what you have done and the skills you have. Remember that the tasks you do at home, at church, and as a volunteer all count.

IT'S NOT A GOOD IDEA TO...

- Bring anything unrelated to the job into the interview; for example, your children, friends, pets, pager, or gym bag.

- It's also not a good idea to be more than 20 minutes early.

- Be rude or ill-mannered toward anyone. Any person in the building could be the boss!

- Pretend to be something you're not. Don't laugh too hard or try too hard to please.

- Exaggerate or lie about your skills or experience. It will only come back to haunt you.

- Mention any legal, financial, personnel problems the company may be having. If these topics do come up, talk positively and optimistically about the company's future.

- Ramble on about a question you've already answered. Give thoughtful answers, but don't waste the interviewer's time with information that's not relevant to the interview.

- Bring up past squabbles or problems with other employers. If the interviewer asks about your previous employers, be as positive as you can, without lying.

- Mention that you have been on public assistance, unless it's relevant or the employer mentions it. Talk about your strengths and experience instead.

Hints for a Successful Interview (*continued*)

IT'S A GOOD IDEA TO...

- Know your salary range. When asked "What are your ideas on salary?" answer with a question for the interviewer, such as "What do you pay people with my skills and experience?"

- Ask questions about such things as the company's plans and the nature of the job. Your questions will indicate interest and motivation.

- Be prepared for the interviewer to say, "You're perfect for this job. When can you start?" Planning what to say will keep you from making a snap decision. Most employers will allow you time to make this decision.

- Thank the interviewer even if they indicate that you are not right for the job. Ask about other companies that might be hiring. Get the name of someone else to see.

- Send a brief thank-you note the day after the interview. Write or type neatly, and briefly restate your interest in the position.

- Call a few days after the interview to see if a hiring decision has been made. Remind the person what job you interviewed for and when he or she spoke with you.

IT'S NOT A GOOD IDEA TO...

- Say a number or a salary range before the interviewer does. After the employer makes the first move and states a salary range or a specific number, you can respond to it. This helps ensure that you get a fair offer.

- Ask about salary and benefits. Doing so gives the impression that you're only interested in money.

- Accept a job immediately if it is offered to you at an interview, unless work needs to begin immediately. Ask if you can think about the offer, talk to your family, and get back with the interviewer the next day. This helps you make a decision you will be happy with.

- Get angry or unpleasant if the employer tells you that you didn't get the job. Be positive and thankful anyway. You may want to apply for a job with the same employer again later!

- Forget about the interview and assume you didn't get the job, even if you feel it didn't go well.

- Be a pest by calling several times over several days. Call once and then wait. If you still don't hear after several more days, call again. Remember to be patient!

Looking Your Best

First impressions are very important when you interview. The way you look can help you get the job you are trying for. Here are a few tips to assist you in getting ready for a job interview.

CLOTHING

Women should wear

- Solid, conservative colors
- A skirt, business dress, pant suit, or blouse and slacks
- Conservative accessories
- No more than one ring per hand
- No dangling earrings
- Clean, ironed, well-fitting clothes

Men should wear

- Solid, conservative colors
- A suit or a blazer/sports jacket
- A tie that is darker than the shirt
- A dress shirt with collar
- Dress shoes that are polished and clean
- A belt that matches the shoes

Before the interview, be sure to bathe and use mouthwash and deodorant.

GROOMING

Women should

- Brush teeth and bathe, using mouthwash and deodorant
- Choose a conservative hairstyle that is not too high or too far out on the sides
- Apply mild, natural makeup, including matching lipstick
- Use moderate amount of perfume or cologne, if any

Men should

- Brush teeth and bathe, using mouthwash and deodorant
- Choose a clean, conservative haircut
- Shave, or wear a neatly trimmed mustache or beard
- Use only moderate amount of cologne, if any

Interview Checklist

Before my interview I will

_____ get a haircut

_____ clean and press my clothes

_____ wash my hands and cut my nails

_____ shower and use deodorant

_____ shine my shoes

_____ trim or shave my beard or mustache

_____ brush my teeth and use mouthwash

_____ use no perfume or after-shave or use only a little

_____ buy a new _____
(for example, an article of clothing, a briefcase, or a portfolio)

_____ be sure my calendar is clear

_____ determine how long it will take me to get to the interview

_____ find out where I should park

_____ be sure I have enough money for transportation and parking

_____ arrange for someone to take me to the interview and be sure they have blocked out enough time

_____ make arrangements for child care

_____ practice answering questions I think I may be asked

I will wear my

_____ suit or dress

_____ shirt or blouse

_____ pants or slacks

_____ tie

_____ belt

_____ socks or stockings

_____ shoes or work boots

_____ jacket or coat

_____ conservative jewelry

_____ purse or briefcase (not both)

_____ conservative makeup

_____ _____

I will bring

_____ a note pad

_____ two pens

_____ my resume

_____ my list of references

_____ my portfolio and work samples

_____ any necessary licenses (for example, heavy equipment, limousine, or bus)

_____ my date book or daily planner

_____ my application

_____ my research

_____ questions

Questions You Might Be Asked During a Job Interview

Here is a list of questions an interviewer might ask you. Think about how you will answer these questions, then practice answering them aloud.

- What do you know about our company? (Use what you learned when you researched the company.)

- What qualifications do you have for this job? (Match what you know about the job and company to your experience.)

- What is your greatest strength? (Relate your strengths to the job description.)

- What is your greatest weakness? (Show how your weaknesses can be positives; for example, indicate that you are a perfectionist with high self-expectations. Admit a past problem and what you learned from it.)

- What can you tell me about yourself? (Reveal something that is somewhat personal but still professional.)

- Why did you leave your previous job(s)? (Turn this into a positive.)

- If you were hired, what ideas and talents could you contribute to the position or to our company?

- What would you do if _____?
  (Imagine situations that test your knowledge of the job.)

- Can you give me an example of how you have demonstrated _____
  skill? (Think first. Be specific. Speak only long enough to answer the question.)

- What example can you give me of how you handled a difficult situation on a previous job?

- Why are you interested in working for this company? (Relate your skills to what you know about the company.)

- What related education do you have? (Use examples that show how your education relates to the position.)

- Why have you chosen this particular field?

- How would you describe your best/worst boss? (Be positive, not critical.)

- In a job, what interests you most/least? (Show how your interests are related to the position.)

- How do others describe you? (Keep your response positive.)

- What do you consider the single most important idea you contributed or your most noteworthy accomplishment in your last job?

- Where do you see yourself in three years? (Demonstrate ambition and flexibility.)

- How does this position fit into your future plans? (Demonstrate potential and ambition.)

- What could you have done better on your last job? (Be positive.)

- What have you done recently that shows your initiative and willingness to work?

- How would you describe yourself to others? (Be positive and brief.)

Answering Questions About Being on Welfare

In an interview, an employer may ask you to discuss your recent work-related activities. If you have not been working and have been on public assistance, these questions may be awkward and difficult to answer.

The key is to be honest about your past and present situation. Also, be optimistic and enthusiastic about the future. Show the employer that being on public assistance does not mean that you are lazy or unskilled. Use your attitude and abilities to prove that you are a skilled worker who can be beneficial to the employer.

Following are a few suggestions for dealing with questions about your work history and your time on public assistance. Remember to be honest with yourself and with the employer!

- I haven't been working for the past two years. I was down on my luck for awhile and had to turn to public assistance for help. While on welfare, I've learned to manage my time and my money very well. I've run a house of four people on a very limited budget. I've managed my children's school and activity schedules. And I've been practicing my typing and writing skills. I'm really excited about getting back to work and learning new skills. I'm ready to grow as a person and as a professional.

- I've been unable to find a job lately, but I have been volunteering at my church. I've been working on a fund-raising campaign to buy new pews and a small play gym for the children. Doing this has taught me to keep a budget, talk to strangers, be enthusiastic all the time, and love to work. I'm really glad to have the opportunity now to get a full-time job.

- My work experience recently hasn't been great, but I have spent a lot of time fixing up my house. And I even helped my neighbor redecorate her bathroom. I put in the new light and water fixtures for her. Construction is what I love. Even when I'm not working, I just can't stop doing it!

- Being on welfare has taught me a lot about money and the importance of work. I've learned how good it is to have a job and get a regular paycheck. I used to work as a secretary for a small manufacturing company. I was great at answering the phones, typing, filing, and keeping the office organized. I miss the satisfaction I got from working, and I'm looking forward to working again.

- It was hard for me to not be working. After I got my children off to school and cleaned the house, I would go to the library to research companies I wanted to work for and jobs I wanted to have. That's how I found out about you. This company seems perfect for where I want to be. I think my clerical skills and enthusiasm are just right for this office!

Questions *You* Might Want to Ask During a Job Interview

You can add questions as you research careers and companies. Choose just 3 or 4 questions to ask during an interview.

- How do you feel about working in this organization?

- Were there any questions that I didn't adequately answer?

- What aspects of this job could be performed better in the future than they have been in the past?

- What are the key challenges or problems of this position?

- Where are the opportunities for advancement here, assuming I meet or exceed the job's responsibilities?

- What are your company's short- and long-term objectives?

- When will a decision be made about this position?

- What do you see as my greatest strengths and weaknesses pertaining to this position?

- What are the opportunities here for personal growth?

- What makes your firm different from its competitors?

- What do you see as the company's strengths and weaknesses?

- How would you describe your corporation's personality and management style?

- What is the overall structure of the department where this position is located?

- What characteristics does a successful person within your company possess?

FOLLOWING UP AFTER AN INTERVIEW

After you have an interview for a job, you should send a thank-you note to the person who interviewed you. You should also take some time to think about how the interview went, what you need to do to follow up with the employer, and what you learned from the experience.

Ronald Morgan
123 Main Street, Apt. C-3
St. Paul, MN 55050
(123) 123-4567

> **Sample Thank-You Note**

January 19, 20XX

Mr. Vincent Kelger
Research and Development Manager
Computers International
11234 West Ivanto Avenue
St. Paul, MN 55051

Dear Mr. Kelger:

Thank you for the time you spent reviewing and discussing my skills in relation to the Computer Analyst position. I enjoyed learning more about your company and your plans for the future.

The position sounds very interesting, particularly because it would give me an opportunity to use my abilities and experience in computer programming and troubleshooting.

I will call you in a few days in the hope that you have reached a decision favorable to both of us.

Sincerely,

Ronald Morgan

Ronald Morgan

Post-Interview Checklist

Company name: _____   Date of interview: _____

Interviewer's name: _____

Date to call back: _____   Date of decision: _____

Was I on time?   Yes _____   No _____

Did I dress appropriately?   Yes _____   No _____

Do I need to send additional information?

- resume or application   Yes _____   No _____
- reference list/reference letters   Yes _____   No _____
- work samples   Yes _____   No _____

Did I give a positive indication of my interest in the job?   Yes _____   No _____

Did I mention who referred me?   Yes _____   No _____

What was the interviewer's general impression of my resume? _____

_____

What was discussed the most? _____

_____

What did the employer seem particularly interested in? _____

_____

What questions did I have the most difficulty answering? _____

_____

What questions did I answer most effectively? _____

_____

What further information did I obtain about the company by asking questions?

_____

What can I do to improve my effort? _____

_____

Learning From Experience

Turn every interview into a positive experience. Even if you don't get the job you were applying for, take a hard look at what happened and learn from it. Use the information below to guide you in your preparation for your next interview.

Reasons for Rejection	_Ways to Control_
Poor personal appearance, careless dress	Follow grooming and dressing guidelines
Lack of enthusiasm and interest	Express enthusiasm with my voice, talk with energy and optimism
Lack of clear goals or ambition	Link my skills to the position, emphasize where I want my career to go
Poor speech habits, inability to express myself	Practice answering questions so I use good grammar and improve my presentation
Lack of preparation, failure to research the company, inability to ask intelligent questions or make intelligent comments	Research the company and practice answering informed questions about it
Failure to look at interviewer or demonstrate interest	Always look the interviewer in the eye and nod with interest at the interviewer's comments
Unrealistic salary demands or more interest in salary than in opportunity	Research and discuss a realistic salary
Inability to relate skills and knowledge to job, indefinite responses to questions	Prepare and practice answers to expected questions, emphasize my skills
Negative comments about previous employers or obvious dislike for various types of authority	Consider and practice answers about work experience and my relationship with previous supervisors and employers
Lack of interest in the company or industry	Research the company and industry
Weak excuses or hedging about unfavorable information in my background	Admit my mistakes, talk about learning from them, and present a positive picture
Unwillingness to start where needed and work my way up	Stress that I want the job and am willing to make a commitment
Lack of knowledge in specialized areas	Practice answers to expected questions so I can show my relevant knowledge
Poor attitude, as shown by being rude or negative, showing prejudice, or having low moral standards	Consider how I present myself, think before I speak

SECTION

4

Success That Lasts

The previous sections of this workbook gave you information to use while looking for a job. This section will help you be successful in your job after you are hired. It covers these topics:

- **Getting Ready to Work:** You will think about how to prepare for your first day on the job.

- **Tips for Lasting Success on the Job:** You will look at several brief suggestions for being a successful and happy employee.

GETTING READY TO WORK

When you start your job, you want to arrive on time and be ready to work. Think about the following items. Check off each item as you take care of it. In the spaces at the bottom, you can write in other items you think of.

Before your first day of work

❑ Set your alarm clock

❑ Choose a clean, professional outfit to wear

❑ Make transportation plans, including getting a bus pass, setting aside money for gas and parking, or making carpool arrangements

❑ Make a back-up transportation plan

❑ Arrange for daycare needs

❑ Make a back-up daycare plan

❑ Decide how your children will get home from school or daycare

❑ Make a back-up plan for how your children will get home

❑ Prepare a sack lunch or set aside money for lunch

❑ _____

❑ _____

TIPS FOR LASTING SUCCESS ON THE JOB

- Keep personal phone calls brief.

- Know your work schedule and be at work when you are scheduled.

- Have a back-up plan for emergencies.

- Try to see things from your employer's point of view.

- Call your employer if you know you are going to be late or if you have a conflict.

- Be sure you get to work and get there on time.

- Pay special attention to being prompt for the first six months.

- Ask for more work when your work is complete.

- Remember that you are not the only person who can do your job.

- Repeat to your supervisor what your supervisor asks you to do, to be sure you understand what the task is and how to do it.

- Ask questions about what you do not understand.

- Remember that you are at work. Watch your language and your attitude.

- Treat everyone with respect.

- Avoid office politics. Keep information confidential and don't gossip.

- Be willing to share your ideas and opinions.

- Be a team player. Listen more and talk less.

- Know what is and is not appropriate to talk about in the work place.

- Know when it is appropriate to offer suggestions and give input.

- Think of work-related emergencies before they occur. Keep a list of solutions handy.

- Have fun! Doing so helps you remain interested, positive, and excited about your work and makes you a better worker and a happier person.